I CAN TALK
WITH GOD

Written and Illustrated by
Helen Caswell

Abingdon Press
Nashville

Library of Congress Cataloging-in-Publication Data

Caswell, Helen Rayburn.
  I can talk with God / written and illustrated by Helen Caswell.
    p. cm. — (Growing in faith series)
  Summary: A young child talks to God about a variety of things throughout the day.
  ISBN 0-687-18686-2 (pbk. : alk. paper)
  1. Prayer—Juvenile literature. [1. Prayer.] I. Title.
  II. Series.
  BV212.C37 1989
  248.3'2—dc19   88-30629
                                                              CIP
                                                              AC

MANUFACTURED IN HONG KONG

I can talk with God.

In the morning when I get up,
I thank God for the new day,
even if it's raining.

I thank God for my orange juice and cereal and my toast with jelly on it.

Some days I feel so happy I just have to jump up and down and thank God for the whole world
and especially me
and everything.

I ask God to take care of all of us.
I ask God for lots of things.
Sometimes the answer is yes, and sometimes the answer is no,
and sometimes God doesn't seem to answer me at all.

But maybe that's because I don't
listen well enough.
You have to listen very carefully,
because God doesn't talk to you like
your parents,
or your sister, or anybody.

God answers you inside your head.
When I say, "Make my little sister good,"
I hear a little voice inside my head that
makes me think, "My little sister copies me,
so I have to be good *first*."

When I asked God for a pony,
the little voice said, "Where would you put it?"

If I feel sad or if I feel angry,
I talk to God about it, and then I feel better.

Sometimes it helps to get down on my knees and hold my hands together and close my eyes. Sometimes it's nice to pray with other people—lots of people all talking to God at once.

But best of all is when I'm in bed at night, in the dark,
and nobody's there but God and me,
and I can talk with God.

God Must Like to Laugh teaches children about God and the world God created.

THE GROWING IN·FAITH LIBRARY

The Growing in Faith Library presents these beautifully illustrated books by Helen Caswell. They are designed to introduce children to six basic concepts of the Christian faith.

I Can Talk with God shows children how they can pray and listen to God.

I Know Who Jesus Is tells children about Jesus and his life.

Also available is the **Guidebook for Adults**—for parents, grandparents, and teachers who love their three- to seven-year-olds and want them to grow in faith.

The **Guidebook** uses each of the six books to

- Address children's questions
- Identify teachable moments
- Give additional ideas to help children grow in faith

God's Love Is for Sharing explains how we can share God's love with others.

My Big Family at Church helps children understand church and why we go.

God Is Always with Me helps children understand eternal life.